CURSIVE HANDWRITING WORKBOOK FOR TEENS

CURSIVE HANDWRITING WORKBOOK

For Teens

EXERCISES TO LEARN, PRACTICE, & IMPROVE

MISSY BRIGGS

ILLUSTRATION BY JACINTA KAY

ROCKRIDGE
PRESS

For Rusty and Chica

For general information on our other products and services or to obtain technical support, please contact our Customer Care Department within the United States at (866) 744-2665, or outside the United States at (510) 253-0500.

Rockridge Press publishes its books in a variety of electronic and print formats. Some content that appears in print may not be available in electronic books, and vice versa.

TRADEMARKS: Rockridge Press and the Rockridge Press logo are trademarks or registered trademarks of Callisto Media Inc. and/or its affiliates, in the United States and other countries, and may not be used without written permission. All other trademarks are the property of their respective owners. Rockridge Press is not associated with any product or vendor mentioned in this book.

Interior and Cover Designer: Monica Cheng
Art Producer: Sara Feinstein
Editor: Eliza Kirby
Production Editor: Nora Milman
Production Manager: Riley Hoffman

Illustration © 2021 Jacinta Kay. Author photo courtesy of Jessica Lopez.

ISBN: Print 978-1-64876-839-2
R1

CONTENTS

INTRODUCTION

Cursive writing is like a secret code. I remember pulling letters out of the mailbox when I was eight. Even though I could read, I couldn't make out every word on the envelope. The day I was introduced to cursive writing in third grade, I entered the secret club. I've been in love with cursive writing, lettering, and calligraphy ever since. My college studies in art history took me on a journey from ancient Egyptian hieroglyphics all the way to the Phoenicians and their alphabet—which is similar to the one we use today. Having had formal training in calligraphy and typography, I taught myself the art of modern brush lettering. I still teach online and in-person brush-lettering workshops to thousands of students. Now my own kids are making their way through upper elementary and middle school, and it's clear that typing has taken over as a main form of written communication. Many schools no longer teach cursive, since it is not a part of the Common Core standards, but you can still take time to incorporate it into your daily life. That's where this book comes in.

In these pages, you'll find step-by-step introductions to each letter in the cursive alphabet, both lower- and uppercase. There is practice space for each letter and for joining the letters to make words. You will also practice short passages and quotes to help you build up confidence in your skills. Cursive writing is an easy way to write faster than you can print, and it has lots of practical benefits. Did you know that you learn and remember things better when you write by hand versus typing or just reading? And writing thank-you notes for a gift or after an interview will go much more quickly once you've mastered cursive writing. Learning cursive opens the door to creative pursuits like bullet journaling, calligraphy, and hand lettering. Maybe you'll fall in love with putting pen to paper and start writing a novel by hand! Maybe you'll want to learn more about the design of letters and how to create different alphabet styles. So many new opportunities await!

Flip through the book and check out all the practice pages. If you're like me and you prefer not to write directly in a book, you're in luck. Downloadable and printable pdfs of all the practice pages are available at CallistoMediaBooks.com/cursiveforteens. Just download, print, and practice—and keep practicing. You will never feel as though you are finished or that this book has been *used up* after you've been through the exercises once.

HOW TO USE THIS BOOK

This book is broken down into three chapters. Chapter 1 will introduce you to the mechanics of cursive handwriting. You will discover reasons why it's so important to learn cursive, common barriers to success and how to overcome them, how to set up your practice space, how to find proper pencils and pens to use, and even how to hold your pencil or pen. Chapter 2 is where you will actually begin to learn and practice writing cursive letters. There will be plenty of space and opportunities to practice individual letters and also words and sentences. Chapter 3 is dedicated to more practice, including how to use cursive for your signature and to write a quick thank-you note. A bonus section at the end includes ways to get really creative with your new skills. You'll learn about bullet journaling, hand lettering, and brush calligraphy and how they are related to cursive writing.

The best way to work through this book is from beginning to end. The practice pages are set up to build skills one upon the next. Individual letters with arrows will show you how to form each letter—both uppercase and lowercase. Don't feel as though you need to work through the entire alphabet in one sitting. You can break your practice down into increments that feel doable and fit into your schedule. If cursive practice becomes tedious or a dreaded task, you're not going to find it enjoyable, and you'll likely give up. Instead, set aside 10 to 15 minutes per day and work through the book one page at a time. Work on learning to form each of the lowercase letters first, then progress to uppercase letters. Don't spend too much time perfecting each letter before moving on to joining letters to form words. You don't often write a single lowercase letter without joining it to another, so practicing a letter endlessly on its own doesn't make sense. That said, if you find you are having issues remembering how to form a letter properly, go back and practice that specific letter before returning to practice with words and phrases.

Over time, you will see tremendous improvement in your cursive. As with any new skill, practice is required. Your first attempts may seem shaky, but you will see improvement day by day. If you have downloaded and printed the practice sheets, write the date at the top of your paper before you get started. Your skills will get stronger as you go, and it's fun to look back and see progression over time. If you were introduced to cursive in elementary school, you're ahead of the game here. But if you weren't, don't worry. We're going to take this step-by-step, so you will feel confident in your cursive writing skills.

1

CURSIVE HANDWRITING 101

Welcome to your introduction to cursive hand-writing! Your journey has just begun. This chapter will offer an overview of why cursive writing is helpful and useful. You will discover some common challenges that you may face along the way. And spoiler alert: Many people face these challenges, so you're not alone. Finally, you'll learn about setting up your workspace and the materials you need in order to get started.

Why Cursive?

Throughout history, writing styles have been closely connected to the materials available. Early writing on papyrus with reed pens was the result of the most efficient way to make a mark using those tools. The advancement of modern technology means that we are no longer limited by tools. We can use ballpoint pens and pencils to draw letters in any way we choose. This also means that we've come to use computers and phones for a lot of our written communication. You may even be more comfortable typing than writing!

Still, that doesn't mean writing by hand is totally useless. In fact, studies suggest that college students taking notes by hand are more likely to remember material for exams. Cursive is a great option for note taking—since letters are joined, it's the quickest method of writing by hand.

There are more uses for cursive than just taking notes. As you study history, you may come across primary sources written in cursive. You'll also use cursive to sign your name on documents, to fill out applications and forms, and to respond to snail-mail correspondence. And cursive will come in handy as you read signs, letters, and notes. Forget learning to write in cursive; let's avoid the possible embarrassment of not being able to *read* a cursive note from your boss or teacher one day.

Aa Bb Cc Dd

Ee Ff Gg Hh

Ii Jj Kk Ll

Mm Nn Oo

Pp Qq Rr

Ss Tt Uu Vv

Ww Xx Yy Zz

Common Challenges

Learning a new skill like cursive can present challenges, from finding the time to practice to having trouble with letter formation. Here are a few tips to combat common problems.

Practice Time

A common challenge that affects all students is lack of time and opportunity to practice, especially if your school doesn't teach cursive. A quick fix would be to set aside time while doing homework specifically to practice cursive handwriting. Add a page or two from this book to your daily schedule to get into the habit.

Letter Formation

If you're having trouble forming letters, you may want to practice letters in the groupings suggested below. These groupings contain letters with similar shapes, not in alphabetical order.

LOWERCASE LETTER PRACTICE GROUPING

Group 1.   *a, c, d, g, o, p, q*

Group 2.   *b, e, f, h, k, l*

Group 3.   *m, n, v, x, y, z*

Group 4.   *i, j, r, s, t,*
u, w

UPPERCASE LETTER PRACTICE GROUPING

Group 1. $\mathcal{A}, \mathcal{C}, \mathcal{D}, \mathcal{E}, \mathcal{O}, \mathcal{Q}$

Group 2. $\mathcal{H}, \mathcal{K}, \mathcal{M}, \mathcal{N}, \mathcal{U}, \mathcal{V}$
              $\mathcal{W}, \mathcal{X}, \mathcal{Y}, \mathcal{Z}$

Group 3. $\mathcal{G}, \mathcal{I}, \mathcal{J}, \mathcal{L}, \mathcal{S}$

Group 4. $\mathcal{F}, \mathcal{T}$

Group 5. $\mathcal{B}, \mathcal{P}, \mathcal{R}$

The practice exercises in this book contain words that are commonly used. Shift your focus to the most commonly used letters and words as a way to make the most of your time and effort. Once you learn how to form a lowercase q, there's no need to practice it as often as a lowercase e.

Lefties

I'm a lefty, too! You're not alone. Left-handed writers may find cursive and the natural flow of letters from one to the other to be a challenge. Maybe your grip or hand position prevents you from seeing your work clearly. Lefties should consider adjusting their seated position in any way that means they don't have to crane their neck to see their work clearly. This might mean shifting your chair so your left hip is close to the desk, allowing a clear view. Quick-drying pens are also a good idea to avoid smudges and smearing of ink. Interesting fact: Hooked-grip lefties hold their arm over their writing. They can see their work clearly *under* their hand, and the motion of writing across a page is a pulling motion, much like it is for a righty. If you write this way, disregard anything that is suggested for lefties. You're basically a righty.

Learning Disabilities

It's important to note that you may have more trouble learning cursive if you deal with a learning disability like dysgraphia, dyslexia, dyspraxia, or ADHD. These are very common; they affect one in five students in the United States. A learning disability does not prevent you from learning cursive handwriting, but it can slow down your progress. If you're having trouble, a parent, teacher, or therapist may be able to help you out.

Setting Up for Success

The first step in learning cursive handwriting is to create an optimal writing environment. This does not mean you need a lot of space! You only need enough room for this book and a sheet of practice paper. If you prefer to write on a flat surface instead of directly in this book, you can download and print practice pages. Downloadable pages from this book are available at CallistoMediaBooks.com/cursiveforteens.

Your Practice Space

A good handwriting practice space should be well-lit, uncluttered, and free of distractions. Put away any electronics that might distract you. Turn on quiet music if it helps you relax and focus. Set up the desk or table space so that you are able to sit with your back straight and feet on the floor. Think of elongating your spine from your waist up to the top of your head, and relax your shoulders. Lean forward slightly in your seat so that your forearms and wrists can rest lightly on the table with your arms at a 90-degree angle. If you are unable to sit in this position with your feet flat on the floor, place a stool or several books under your feet.

Papers, Pencils, and Pens

It might seem unimportant, but the position of your paper can make a big difference. Your cursive handwriting should flow smoothly across the paper, and the position of the paper can affect how easily your arm guides the writing across the page. For right-handed students, this means having the paper at an angle tilted 45 degrees to the left. For left-handed students, this means turning your paper 45 degrees to the right. If you start writing with the paper turned this way and your hand or wrist position doesn't feel comfortable, consider turning your paper a little more or less. Try tracing some sample lettering or warm-up exercises in this book to ensure that you can trace without feeling the need to adjust your body. Next, choose your preferred writing tool. Either a pencil or a pen will work well; just be sure that it writes smoothly. Choose pencils with a balanced HB or 2B graphite. A standard #2 yellow pencil has this type of balanced graphite. Pencils that have soft graphite will require too-frequent sharpening. Ballpoint pens or gel pens have ink that flows smoothly. They're better choices than felt-tipped pens for practice.

 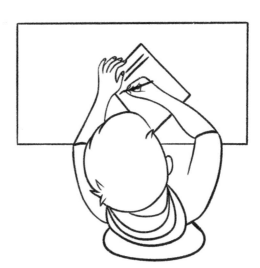

DIFFERENT HAND HOLDS

The way you hold your writing tool has an effect on your writing. It can impact the length of time you can write comfortably as well as overall legibility. There is no right or wrong way to grip your pen, but grasping in a way that is not recommended can cause fatigue or calluses to develop.

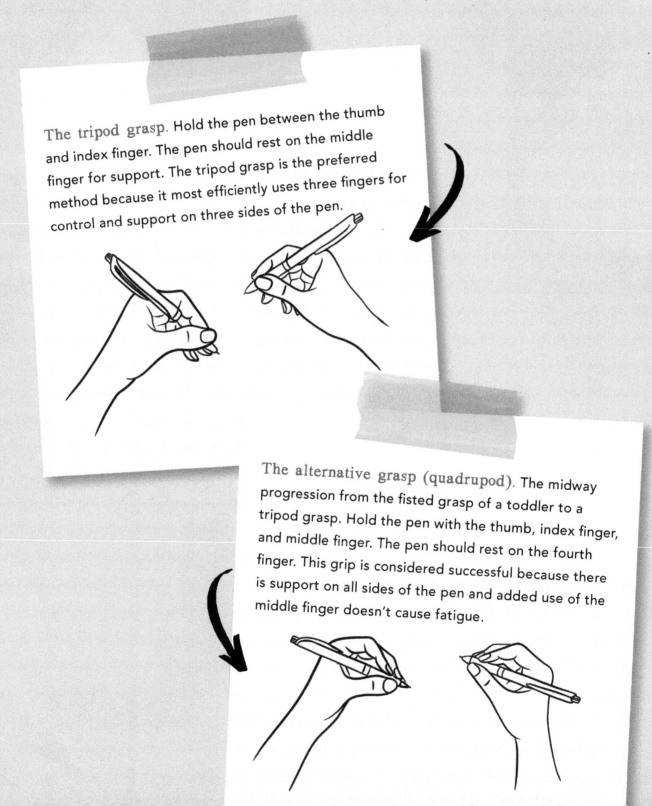

The tripod grasp. Hold the pen between the thumb and index finger. The pen should rest on the middle finger for support. The tripod grasp is the preferred method because it most efficiently uses three fingers for control and support on three sides of the pen.

The alternative grasp (quadrupod). The midway progression from the fisted grasp of a toddler to a tripod grasp. Hold the pen with the thumb, index finger, and middle finger. The pen should rest on the fourth finger. This grip is considered successful because there is support on all sides of the pen and added use of the middle finger doesn't cause fatigue.

The adapted tripod (left) and the thumb wrap (right). Grasps preferred to aid in stability. Perhaps your finger strength wasn't enough to feel successful with a tripod grasp, and this just "felt right." If you use these or any other similar pen grasp, it's likely that it has been cemented as a habit that would be hard to break. Remember, what's most important is that a pen grasp is functional and does not cause pain or fatigue. These grasps are not necessarily bad or incorrect.

Tips for "death grip": My pen grasp is unconventional. I'm left-handed and I hold the pen vertically, grasping with five fingers. Over time, this developed into an issue where gripping the pen tightly caused fatigue. The remedy is to try to relieve pressure. Try holding a stress ball in the opposite hand. Putting pressure on your opposite hand will cause your dominant hand to release pressure. Another tip is to try pens or pencils that have a larger barrel. A thicker pen is more difficult to grip tightly.

2

PRACTICE MAKES PERFECT

Now that you've gotten your setup ready, let's jump into practicing cursive. You'll begin with some warm-ups and move on to real letters from there. The mechanics of cursive writing are all about connecting letters to improve speed. The real speed comes later, but just limiting the number of times you lift the pen off the page will automatically make you write faster.

Warm-Ups: Scribbles and Strokes

It's important to relax and warm up before you begin cursive writing. This is different from the way you've written before, so it's crucial to start with a clear intention to make smooth strokes across the page. To begin, sit up straight at your desk or table with your feet flat on the floor. Take a few deep breaths and raise your arms up into the air. Stretch upward or out to the side. Now release the stretch and shake out your hands. Pick up your pen lightly and work through the warm-ups across the next two pages. Focus on your posture and pen grip as you work, rather than on making the marks exactly right. Work slowly through the practice. This is not the time to pick up speed. These are good exercises to loosen your grip and prepare for cursive letters.

Lowercase Letters

This section will focus entirely on the formation of lowercase letters. Each letter is illustrated with arrows and numbers. The directional arrows show the order of letter formation, not the number of pen strokes. You can pause when changing direction without lifting your pen from the paper, but where there is a curve, make it in one continuous stroke. Take your time to work through each letter slowly.

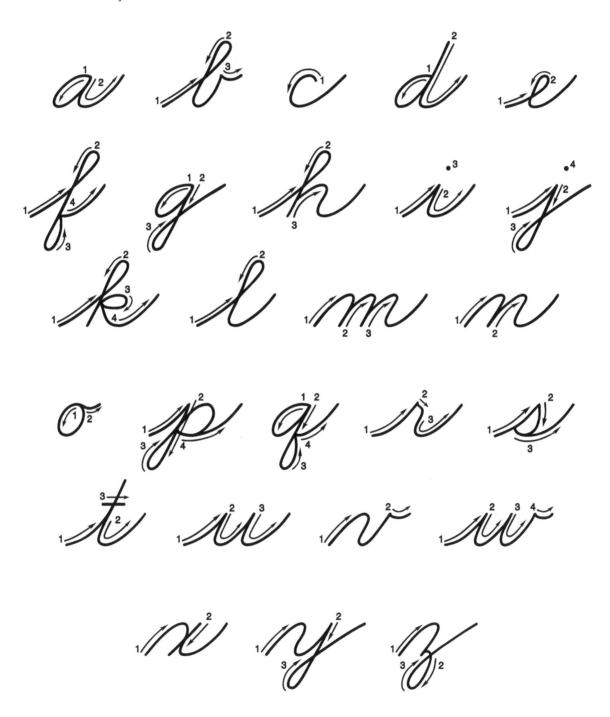

a   a a

a   aa aa

b   b b

b   bb ba

c   c c

c   cc ca

d   d d

d   dd da

e   e e

e   ee ea

f   f f

f   ff fe

g   g g

g   gg ge

h   h h

h   hh he

i i

ii ii

j j

jj je

k k

kk ke

l l

ll le

m   m m

m   mm me

m   n m

m   nn ne

o   o o

o   oo oe

p   p p

p   pp po

q q

q q qu

r r

r r ro

s s

ss so

t t

tt to

u u

uuu uo

v v

vu vu

w w

wwu wu

x x

xx xu

Y *Y*

Yy *Yu*

Z *Z*

Zy *Zu*

Capital Letters

Let's move on to capital letters. Just like in the lowercase practice, each capital letter is illustrated with numbers and arrows to help guide you in the direction and order of formation. These can look intimidating because they have more steps. Work slowly and confidently through each one, and soon they will just flow off your pen!

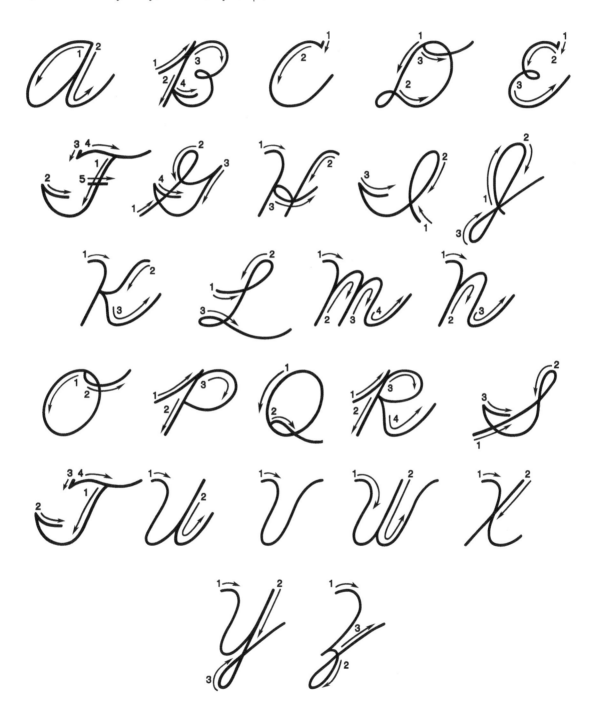

a a

Aa Ae

B B

Ba Be

C C

Ca Ce

D D

Da De

E E

Ea Ee

F F

Fa Fe

G G

Ga Ge

H H

Ha He

l l

la le

J J

Je Ji

K K

Ke Ki

L L

Le Li

M *M*

Me Mi

n n

ne ni

O O

Oi Oo

P P

Pi Po

Q Q

Qi Qu

R R

Ri Ro

S S

Si So

T T

Ti To

$\mathcal{U}$

$\mathcal{U}$ *Uu*

$\mathcal{U}$ *Ui Uo*

$\mathcal{V}$ *Vv*

$\mathcal{V}$ *Vo Vu*

$\mathcal{W}$ *Ww*

$\mathcal{W}$ *Wo Wu*

$\mathcal{X}$ *Xx*

$\mathcal{X}$ *Xo Xu*

Y Y

Yo Yu

Z Z

Zo Zu

SAME BUT DIFFERENT

Some capital and lowercase letters in the cursive alphabet look almost the same. To differentiate these when writing, pay attention to sizing or small differences in the way the letters are formed. Letters like A, C, M, N, O, U, V, W, Y, and Z have capital and lowercase letters that look similar. For these letters, pay special attention to writing them at the correct scale. A capital A that is written too small can easily be confused with a lowercase a.

Letters like capital I and lowercase l and e can also be confused. Guidelines and exact details, like the extra stroke at the left of the capital I, will help differentiate them.

Still, other letters like m, n, u, and w can be confused if they are not written properly.

Pay attention to individual letter formation now, and it will be easier to avoid these simple mistakes once you start joining letters.

Capitals and lowercase letters can be confused when not written at the proper size

Aa Cc Nn Oo Uu
Vv Ww Yy Zz

I, l, and e look similar

I l e

Simple M / N, m / n mistakes

M N   m n

Simple U / W mistakes

U W   u w

Joins

A join is the connecting line between two letters. You may not have realized it, but you've already been practicing a join in the letter section. For most letter connections, the join is a natural flowing line between two letters. Other letter joins are trickier and require extra practice. The connection between two lowercase *l*'s is simple because the next *l* begins where the first one ends, or a low join. Two lowercase *a*'s are trickier because you need to exit near the baseline and jump up to where the next *a* begins, retracing your mark a bit to form the next *a*. Joins between letters like *b* and *o* are even trickier because the exit stroke on those letters is up higher, on the waistline, or a high join.

ASCENDER LINE

WAISTLINE

BASELINE

DESCENDER LINE

*The simple low join of two **l**'s (baseline exit to baseline entrance), the trickier join of two **a**'s (baseline exit to waistline entrance), and the more complicated high join of two **o**'s (waistline exit to waistline entrance).*

JOIN AT WAISTLINE

ASCENDER LINE

WAISTLINE

BASELINE

DESCENDER LINE

JOIN AT BASELINE

*The word **joined** has complicated connections like the **j** to the **o**, which requires coming up to the start of the **o** and retracing part of the left side as your pen writes it counterclockwise. The exit from the **o** into the **i** is a high join at the waistline. The rest of the connections are low and flow naturally from the exit at the baseline of one letter into the beginning of the next letter that begins at the baseline.*

Exercise 1

Practice connecting the following letters that have simple low joins. These letters both begin and end with a connecting stroke that comes from the baseline.

Practice letters: e, f, h, i, j, k, l, m, n, p, r, s, t, u, x, y, z

pen

fun

hip

junk

full

lens

silk

puns

sink

flex

zip

yes

test

zest

fix

set

yum

Exercise 2

Practice connecting letters that have more complicated joins. These connections involve some retracing, like connecting *a* to *d*, or exit points that require a high join on the waistline, like *b*, *o*, *v*, or *w*.

Practice letters: a, c, d, g, o, q

ago

dad

cog

cod

cad

age

dock

goad

gain

aqua

duct

goat

quad

acquit

adjoin

adapt

dogged

drool

good

again

equip

acquire

racquet

acquaint

lacquer

edge

Practice letters: b, o, v, w

bow

vow

wow

bob

wobble

oven

void

bowl

avow

owe

over

own

vote

boat

owl

cobweb

sob

cover

HELPFUL TIPS

For Everyone

1. **Prioritize practice.** If you're struggling with certain letters, practice those first.

2. **Fight fatigue.** Take frequent breaks, if possible. If you're practicing for a long time, stand up at least once an hour and walk around for a minute or two.

3. **Relieve hand cramps.** Ensure you are writing using whole-arm motions and not just finger muscles. Keep your wrist straight, with your arm resting lightly on the table or desk. Check for correct posture as discussed in chapter 1.

For Lefties

1. **Avoid lefty smudge.** To avoid ink stains on the side of your hand, invest in some quick-drying gel pens like Pentel EnerGel-X Retractable Gel Pen. Use an HB or #2 pencil. Don't use pencils that are labeled 4B (or higher, like a 6B or 8B). These are for drawing, and their soft graphite smears.

2. **Keep it in view.** Try to position your hand below the baseline. This will allow a clear view of what you're writing without straining your neck to see under your left hand.

3. **Tilt your paper.** If you prefer to write with your hand directly to the left of your work, tilt your paper even farther clockwise to the right. This will save you from straining your head to the right to see under your hand.

4. **Take breaks.** It's okay to take extra breaks. Consider this: The natural motion of your fingers is to grasp things and pull inward toward your palm. Left-handed writers do the opposite motion. They push the pencil out ahead of their hand. As a lefty, you're doing more work than a righty. Righties drag the pen behind their hand using whole-arm strength and flexing fingers toward the palm, while you're pushing the pen and extending fingers outward. This is more strenuous, so give yourself a break!

Writing for Consistency

To keep your handwriting consistent means that your letters will look similar every time. Your goal should be legibility for your reader. The key to writing consistently correct letters is to match the four Ss: shape, size, spacing, and slope. By practicing on the preceding pages, you should have gained a good knowledge of the shape and size of each letter. Spacing between words and letters should be equal. And the slope should be at the same angle. You probably won't be pulling out a protractor every time you write in cursive, but it's good to get a sense of the ideal angle. All letters should similarly *lean* to the right.

EQUAL SPACING
BETWEEN LETTERS

DOWNWARD STROKES
FOLLOW SAME SLANT LINE

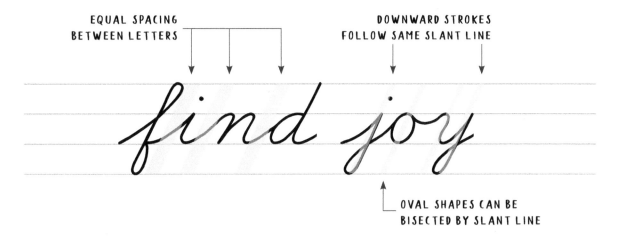

OVAL SHAPES CAN BE
BISECTED BY SLANT LINE

Taking the time to evaluate your work now will ensure consistent writing in the future. As you practice the words and sentences on the following pages, pay attention to the four Ss: the shape, size, spacing, and slope of your cursive handwriting.

Words

In this section, you will practice using joins to form more words. While practicing, note where the joins are easier and where they are more difficult. Then impress your friends by knowing a plant name for every letter of the alphabet!

Aloe

Bamboo

Coconut

Dogwood

Echinacea

Foxglove

Gardenia

Hydrangea

Iris

Juniper

Kale

Lychee

Marigold

Nightshade

Orchid

Poppy

Quince

Rose

Sunflower

Tulip

Ursinia

Violet

Wisteria

Xanthisma

Yarrow

Zinnia

Sentences

Forming complete sentences is the next step in your practice. Take your time to work through each example slowly. Careful copying means that you are also anticipating the next letter of each word in order to properly form the join. Notice how you may also write two short words before pausing to go back and dot an *i* or cross a *t*. This means that you're really building up fluency and confidence. You're intuitively thinking ahead as you work.

The secret of getting ahead is getting started. —*author unknown*

I raise up my voice, not so I can shout but so that those without a voice can be heard. —*Malala Yousafzai*

Life was meant to be
lived, and curiosity must
be kept alive. —*Eleanor Roosevelt*

Ideas do not reach
perfection in a day, no
matter how much study
is put upon them.

—*Alexander Graham Bell*

Fight for the things that you care about, but do it in a way that will lead others to join you. —*Ruth Bader Ginsburg*

Do the best you can until you know better. Then when you know better, do better. —*Maya Angelou*

Instruction does much, but encouragement everything. — *Johann Wolfgang von Goethe*

The way to right wrongs is to turn the light of truth upon them —*Ida B. Wells*

Tolerance and compassion are active, not passive states, born of the capacity to listen, to observe and to respect others. —Indira Gandhi

Today's young people—
everywhere I go—they're
so excited and empowered.
We're listening to their
voices. That gives us a
reason to hope. —*Jane Goodall*

Success doesn't come with painting one picture. It results from taking a certain definite line of action and staying with it. —Georgia O'Keeffe

But humanity's greatest
advances are not in
its discoveries—but in
how those discoveries
are applied to reduce
inequity. *—Bill Gates*

Never, ever be afraid to make some noise and get in good trouble, necessary trouble. —*John Lewis*

There's no person in the whole world like you, and I like you just the way you are. —*Fred Rogers*

You don't make progress
by standing on the
sidelines, whimpering
and complaining. You make
progress by implementing
ideas. —Shirley Chisholm

How wonderful it is that no one has to wait, but can start right now to gradually change the world! —*Anne Frank*

Hope is being able to see that there is light despite all of the darkness. —*Desmond Tutu*

Figure out what you like to do. If you like something, you will do your best. —Katherine Johnson

Remember, no effort that we make to attain something beautiful is ever lost. —Helen Keller

Why, sometimes I've believed as many as six impossible things before breakfast. —Lewis Carroll

The better part of one's life consists of his friendships. —Abraham Lincoln

For they can conquer who
believe they can. —*Virgil*

Those who bring
sunshine to the lives of
others cannot keep it from
themselves. —*J. M. Barrie*

Pursuing peace means
rising above one's own
wants, needs, and
emotions. —*Benazir Bhutto*

Everyone you meet just
wants to be seen and
heard. —*Oprah Winfrey*

Reexamine all you have been told in school or church or in any book ... dismiss whatever insults your own soul. —*Walt Whitman*

Pangrams Practice

A pangram is a sentence that uses every letter in the alphabet at least once. In this section, you will continue to practice your cursive by writing sentences using sample pangrams, such as "The quick brown fox jumps over the lazy dog." Three sample pangrams will be given, followed by space to practice. Then come up with your own pangram!

Sphinx of black quartz, judge my vow.

The five boxing wizards jump quickly.

Sixty zippers were quickly picked from the woven jute bag.

Commonly Used Words

A good way to maximize practice time and effort is to review the most commonly used words in the English language. Included in this practice section are the top 35, with the exception of *I* and *a*, which have been covered already.

1. *the*

2. *be*

3. *to*

4. *of*

5. *and*

6. *in*

7. *that*

8. *have*

9. *it*

10. *for*

11. *not*

12. *on*

13. *with*

14. *he*

15. *as*

16. *you*

17. *do*

18. *at*

19. *this*

20. *but*

21. *his*

22. *by*

23. *from*

24. *they*

25. *we*

26. *say*

27. her

28. she

29. or

30. will

31. is

32. was

33. are

34. what

35. there

WHAT'S MUSCLE MEMORY?

Muscle memory is your subconscious memory of a repeated task. A good example of this is learning to play a video game. There is a sequence of events that has to take place in order to successfully master gameplay. Through repeated practice, you train your brain to memorize individual actions. Have you ever started playing an old game after months of not playing it? You might need a minute or two to get back on track, but you're not starting over from scratch. You're still good at the game! The same muscle memory is at work while practicing cursive handwriting.

Building muscle memory while writing means that repeated practice of a difficult letter will help you remember how to write that letter the next time. If you sit down to practice cursive and repeatedly write the word *the*, you memorize not only individual letters but also the connections between them. After a few attempts, you won't have to think about the letters or the connections again. It will just come to you.

Now that you've practiced letters, words, and some sample sentences, let's put it all together. Use these two pages to write a journal entry in cursive.

3

YOUR SIGNATURE STYLE

You have learned a lot of rules so far about how to form letters. Now it's time to break a few rules and create your own signature style. Signing your name to official documents is an important skill, and in some cases, it's required! You will need to sign your name on your driver's license, passport application, rental or mortgage applications, and the back of checks to endorse them. There are new opportunities to sign contracts electronically, but you will still run across instances where you do need to put pen to paper. Let's be sure you have a personal signature style that's uniquely you. Your signature style will change and evolve over time, but for now you'll try something that is unique but still readable.

Sign Your Name

Start by writing your name below, exactly as it should be written. Write it carefully and take your time to form the letters consistently and with good spacing.

Now add your own flair and style. Think of writing the capital letters larger than they should be, adding a swash or flourish off the end of the last letter, or even underlining your name. Your signature should be something you can write neatly but quickly. Throw the rule of absolute accuracy out the window!

The only rule to keep in mind is that you may be asked to sign your name within a box that will then be electronically scanned. This is the case with voter registration and driver's license applications. Be sure that the proportion of your signature is not too tall or too wide. Think of a rectangle that's ½ inch high by 2 inches wide as a guide.

Barack Obama	Barack Obama
Beyoncé	Beyoncé
Camila Cabello	Camila Cabello
Ruth Bader Ginsburg	Ruth Bader Ginsburg
Walt Disney	Walt Disney
Alexander Hamilton	Alexander Hamilton
Toni Morrison	Toni Morrison
Chris Evans	Chris Evans

MAKE IT PERSONAL

Writing notes and cards by hand conveys a message that you care. Sending a text or an email may be quicker, but handwriting a note in cursive means you took the extra time to sit down and put your thoughts to paper, address an envelope, and drop it in the mail. It may seem old-fashioned, but now that also means it's unique. After receiving a special gift, take the time to write a thoughtful note. You can either deliver it by hand or mail it back. The time you took to write it will be appreciated. And if you go on a job interview or ask a teacher to write a reference for you, be sure to write a thank-you note by hand. There's a really simple formula for writing the perfect thank-you note. It should be about three to four sentences—never more. It can go like this: "Thank you for ___. I appreciate your kindness and generosity." Next, add something about the gift that you like or plan to use it for. Add something personal, and close.

Here is an example, for a recommendation.

June 8, 2021

Dear Mrs. Smith,

Thank you again for taking the time to meet with me. I appreciate your letter of recommendation as I apply for the [insert name of scholarship, program, or job]. Your mentorship during this time has been invaluable.

Kind regards,
Missy Briggs

Use the space on these two pages to practice writing a thank-you note in cursive.

Bullet Journaling

A bullet journal is a specific method of journaling developed by author Ryder Carroll. To get started, think of it as a journal to track assignments and to-dos. If you enjoy the free-form writing that a completely blank journal allows, check out some bullet-journaling blogs for inspiration—you can take a look at the Resources (page 82) in this book as a starting point. Your journal can be really minimalist with text only or more elaborate with illustrations. There are no hard-and-fast rules for creating a journal in a dot-grid notebook, but if you get really into the system, it can help you track past, present, and future goals in one neat and organized space. Using your cursive handwriting in a bullet journal is a great way to get thoughts down more quickly and to have a second type of handwriting for variety.

Hand Lettering

Hand lettering is different from cursive handwriting. Cursive handwriting is written, while hand lettering is drawn. Think of block letters or bubble letters. You cannot write them in one continuous motion like you can with cursive handwriting. They are drawn in pencil, then carefully inked over with pen. And then outlines, highlights, or shadows can be added. If you decide to try out hand lettering, your cursive handwriting skills can be helpful for adding interest to your finished piece of art. Product designers, chalkboard lettering artists, and graphic designers often use cursive in their finished work.

Calligraphy

Calligraphy is another artistic expression of writing. There are so many different styles of calligraphy to learn, but all of them involve drawing letters slowly, stroke by stroke. In italic calligraphy, this means that you use a broad-tip pen held at a specific angle to create a variety of thick and thin lines. In brush calligraphy or pointed-pen calligraphy, you use a brush pen, paintbrush, or pen holder with a nib to create thick and thin lines. Using a nib dipped in ink requires knowledge of both how to use the writing instrument and how to form each letter. It's a good idea to start with brush pens and broad-edge markers to begin learning various types of calligraphy. Your cursive handwriting skills will help you understand how to make letter connections in several script styles.

RESOURCES

MY RESOURCES

Instagram.com/missybriggs
My Instagram is full of inspiration for everything about cursive handwriting, lettering, and applications of lettering for your journal or easy crafts.

MissyBriggs.com
My website offers free getting-started guides for brush lettering, tutorials and tips on lettering, and tons of bullet journal and craft inspiration.

***Easy Creative Lettering* by Missy Briggs**
My book on lettering addresses both lettering and brush calligraphy with step-by-step instruction, 10 alphabet styles, and eight projects.

CURSIVE PRACTICE

CallistoMediaBooks.com/cursiveforteens
Extra practice pages from this book are available for free. Download, print, and keep practicing your cursive handwriting.

BULLET JOURNALING

The Bullet Journal Method by Ryder Carroll

The complete organizational method for bullet journaling is outlined in detail to help keep your life organized. It creates a combined wish list, to-do list, and personal diary out of your blank journal pages.

ArcherAndOlive.com/blogs/news

The complete blog of Archer & Olive. This includes downloadable calendar templates, ideas, tips, and tricks for keeping a bullet journal. If you decide to shop with Archer & Olive, use code MISSY10 for 10 percent off notebooks.

CALLIGRAPHY

IAMPETH.com/lessons

The website of the International Association of Master Penmen, Engrossers, and Teachers of Handwriting (IAMPETH) is *the* source for free resources, lessons, and videos to get started with a variety of different calligraphy scripts.

Calligraphy in Ten Easy Lessons by Eleanor Winters

This book tackles the basics of Italian hand calligraphy in an approachable way for beginners.

REFERENCES

Alstad, Zachary, Elizabeth Sanders, Robert D. Abbott, Anna L. Barnett, Sheila E. Henderson, Vincent Connelly, and Virginia W. Berninger. "Modes of Alphabet Letter Production during Middle Childhood and Adolescence: Interrelationships with Each Other and Other Writing Skills." *Journal of Writing Research* 6, no. 3 (February 2015): 199–231. DOI.org/10.17239/jowr-2015.06.03.1.

Askvik, Eva Ose, F. R. (Ruud) van der Weel, and Audrey L. H. van der Meer. "The Importance of Cursive Handwriting over Typewriting for Learning in the Classroom: A High-Density EEG Study of 12-Year-Old Children and Young Adults." *Frontiers in Psychology* (July 28, 2020). DOI.org/10.3389/fpsyg.2020.01810.

Debczak, Michele. "Texas Is the Latest State to Bring Cursive Writing Back to Its School Curriculums." *Mental Floss*, April 11, 2019. MentalFloss.com/article/579623/texas-to-bring-cursive-writing-back-school-curriculum.

Galenson, David W. *Conceptual Revolutions in Twentieth-Century Art*. New York: Cambridge University Press, 2009.

Klass, Perri. "Why Handwriting Is Still Essential in the Keyboard Age." *New York Times*, June 20, 2016. Well.Blogs.NYTimes.com/2016/06/20/why-handwriting-is-still-essential-in-the-keyboard-age.

NOVA. "A to Z: How Writing Changed the World." PBS, September 30, 2020. PBS.org/wgbh/nova/video/a-to-z-how-writing-changed-the-world.

Nunberg, Geoff. "So Longhand: Has Cursive Reached the End of the Line?" NPR, May 31, 2018. NPR.org/2018/05/31/612197167/so-longhand-has-cursive-reached-the-end-of-the-line.

Rueb, Emily S. "Cursive Seemed to Go the Way of Quills and Parchment. Now It's Coming Back." *New York Times*, April 13, 2019. NYTimes.com/2019/04/13/education/cursive-writing.html.

Shapiro, T. Rees. "Cursive Handwriting Is Disappearing from Public Schools." *Washington Post*, April 4, 2013. WashingtonPost.com/local/education/cursive-handwriting-disappearing-from-public-schools/2013/04/04/215862e0-7d23-11e2-a044-676856536b40_story.html.

Missy Briggs is a full-time artist and the author of *Easy Creative Lettering*. She turns creative lettering into an approachable art form for all—especially fellow lefties—and provides demos, tips, and tricks to her loyal following on Instagram at @missybriggs. Follow her to see the weird, bendy thumb. As a professional artist, Missy does freelance lettering design for Fortune 100 companies and is commissioned by luxury retail brands for onsite calligraphy and monogramming. Missy is a graduate of the University of Miami with a degree in art and art history. She lives and works in her never-tidy home studio in Miami, Florida. Visit her website and sign up for freebies at MissyBriggs.com.

CPSIA information can be obtained
at www.ICGtesting.com
Printed in the USA
JSHW031731270621
15901JS00003BA/3